The Countries

Ukraine

Kristin Van Cleaf

ABDO Publishing Company

visit us at
www.abdopublishing.com

Published by ABDO Publishing Company, 8000 West 78th Street, Edina, Minnesota 55439.
Copyright © 2008 by Abdo Consulting Group, Inc. International copyrights reserved in all
countries. No part of this book may be reproduced in any form without written permission from the
publisher. The Checkerboard Library™ is a trademark and logo of ABDO Publishing Company.

Printed in the United States.

Interior Photos: Alamy pp. 5, 11, 13, 18, 27, 35, 36; AP Images p. 9; Corbis pp. 25, 29, 32, 34;
    Getty Images pp. 21, 31; iStockphoto p. 6

Editors: Rochelle Baltzer, Megan M. Gunderson
Art Direction & Maps: Neil Klinepier

Library of Congress Cataloging-in-Publication Data

Van Cleaf, Kristin, 1976-
  Ukraine / Kristin Van Cleaf.
      p. cm. -- (The countries)
  Includes index.
  ISBN 978-1-59928-788-1
  1. Ukraine--Juvenile literature. I. Title.

  DK508.12.V36 2007
  947.7--dc22

                              2007010185

Contents

Dobryj Den'!

Good day from Ukraine! This country is located in eastern Europe. It is the continent's second-largest country after Russia. Even so, it is slightly smaller than the state of Texas.

Ukraine's land is mainly **steppes**. But, the Carpathian Mountains rise in the west. In the south, the Crimean (kreye-MEE-uhn) Peninsula reaches out into the Black Sea. Many types of trees and grasses provide shelter to a variety of animals in Ukraine.

The Ukrainian people have survived a troubled history. Through the years, many countries have controlled Ukraine. Nations such as Russia and the Soviet Union have forced their **culture** on Ukrainians. But the people have held on to their traditions.

Today, Ukraine is independent. Despite past troubles, its culture still flourishes. Folk arts such as embroidery and egg painting remain strong traditions. Ukraine's determined people honor their nation's past and look to its future.

Dobryj den' *from Ukraine!*

Fast Facts

OFFICIAL NAME: Ukraine
CAPITAL: Kiev

LAND
- Area: 233,090 square miles (603,700 sq km)
- Mountain Ranges: Carpathian Mountains, Crimean Mountains
- Highest Point: Mount Hoverlya 6,762 feet (2,061 m)
- Major Rivers: Dnieper, Dniester, Donets

PEOPLE
- Population: 46,299,862 (July 2007 estimate)
- Major Cities: Kiev, Kharkiv, Dnipropetrovs'k
- Official Language: Ukrainian
- Religions: Ukrainian Orthodoxy, Ukrainian Greek Catholicism, Protestantism, Judaism

GOVERNMENT
- Form: Republic
- Head of State: President
- Head of Government: Prime minister
- Legislature: Unicameral Supreme Council
- Nationhood: August 24, 1991

ECONOMY
- Agricultural Products: Wheat, barley, sugar beets, sunflower seeds, vegetables, beef, milk
- Mining Products: Coal, iron ore, manganese, natural gas, salt
- Manufactured Products: Chemicals, clothing, iron, steel, military equipment, food products
- Money: Hryvnia (1 hryvnia = 100 kopiykas)

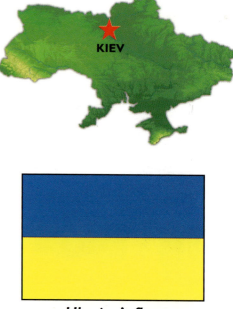

Ukraine's flag

Ukrainian hryvnia

Timeline

4000 to 2000 BC	The Trypillians live in what is now Ukraine
1500 BC	The Cimmerians move into the steppes
AD 882	Oleg, a Norseman, becomes the first ruler of Kievan Rus
980	Prince Vladimir I conquers Kievan Rus
1240	Kievan Rus falls to Mongol Tatars
1387	Poland takes control of Ukraine
1392	Lithuania begins ruling Ukraine
1569	Poland regains control of Ukraine
1648	Bohdan Khmelnytsky leads a Cossack rebellion against the Polish
1795	Russia rules all of Ukraine except Galicia
1917	Ukrainians form the Ukrainian National Republic
1922	Ukraine joins three other nations in forming the Union of Soviet Socialist Republics
1932 to 1933	The Soviet government seizes food from Ukraine; a famine kills more than 5 million Ukrainians
1945	Ukraine helps found the United Nations
1991	Ukraine declares independence from the Soviet Union
1996	The Ukrainian government adopts its new constitution

Uniting Ukraine

What is now Ukraine has continually changed hands for thousands of years. Some of the land's earliest people, the Trypillians, lived there from about 4000 to 2000 BC. They grew crops and made pottery and tools.

By about 1500 BC, the Cimmerians had moved into the **steppes**. The Scythians conquered the Cimmerians about 700 BC. Around this time, Greeks started occupying the northern Black Sea coast.

Between the 200s BC and the AD 1000s, various peoples from surrounding areas controlled the land. As these groups came and went, Slavic tribes moved in from north of the Carpathian Mountains. At Kiev (KEE-ihf), Slavs and Norsemen organized a region called Kievan Rus.

In 882, a Norseman named Oleg became Kievan Rus's first ruler. The kingdom grew to include large areas of the steppes. Prince Vladimir I conquered Kievan Rus in 980. Under his rule, it became a strong nation.

In 1240, Kievan Rus fell to Mongol Tatars. Poland took control in 1387, followed by Lithuania in 1392. When Poland and Lithuania merged in 1569, Poland again ruled Ukraine.

Under Polish and Lithuanian rule, peasants became serfs. They farmed land for their lords but were not free to leave.

Many serfs joined bands of soldiers called Cossacks. In 1648, Bohdan Khmelnytsky (BAWG-dawn kmyehl-NYIHT-skuhih) led a Cossack **rebellion**. He then made a short-lived **alliance**

Today, a monument to Bohdan Khmelnytsky stands near the Cathedral of St. Michael's Golden-Domed Monastery in Kiev.

with Russia against Poland in 1654. After Khmelnytsky died in 1657, the Cossack-controlled land fell into a period of unrest called "the Ruin."

In 1667, Poland and Russia split Ukraine along the Dnieper (NEE-puhr) River. But by 1795, Russia controlled all of Ukraine except Galicia in the west. During the 1800s, Russia outlawed Ukrainian language and **culture**. But Ukrainian culture grew in Galicia, where Austrian rulers were tolerant.

In 1917, **Bolsheviks** led the **Russian Revolution** and overthrew **Czar** Nicholas II. So that year, the Ukrainians formed the Ukrainian National **Republic**. But the Bolsheviks, now called **communists**, seized eastern and central Ukraine in 1920. Poland, Czechoslovakia, and Romania each took parts of the remaining land.

In 1922, Ukraine joined Russia, Transcaucasia, and Belorussia to form the Union of Soviet Socialist Republics. At first, Ukrainian culture was encouraged. But in the 1930s, Soviet ruler Joseph Stalin forced Russian culture and language on the Ukrainians.

At the same time, the communist government began collectivization. This program took people's privately owned farms and combined them into large, state-run farms. Then in 1932 and 1933, the government seized grain and food. This caused a **famine**, which killed more than 5 million Ukrainians.

During **World War II**, Germany occupied nearly all of Ukraine by November 1941. The following year, the Ukrainian Insurgent Army formed to fight both Germany and the Soviet Union. But by October 1944, the **communist** Soviet Union once again controlled Ukraine. More than 5 million Ukrainians died in the war.

In 1945, Ukraine became one of the founding members of the **United Nations**. Meanwhile, the Soviet Union began working to rebuild Ukraine's **economy**. In 1954, it gave Ukraine the Crimean Peninsula as a show of friendship. Despite Ukrainian opposition, the country remained under Soviet control throughout the mid-1900s.

In 1945, British prime minister Winston Churchill, U.S. president Franklin Delano Roosevelt, and Soviet premier Joseph Stalin met on the Crimean Peninsula. There at the Yalta Conference, they discussed the final defeat of Germany.

In April 1986, an accident occurred at the Chernobyl (chuhr-NOH-buhl) **nuclear** power station near Kiev. It released **radioactive** materials into the atmosphere. This killed about 60 people and has led to cancer and other illnesses in Ukraine, Belarus, and Russia. As a result, health experts believe thousands more will die.

In the 1980s, Ukraine's **economy** weakened. Many of the large, state-run farms were wasting resources and money. So, the government began allowing more private ownership.

At the same time, a nationalist movement was growing. Ukrainians wanted more control over their government, economy, and **culture**. So in 1990, the country's **parliament** declared state sovereignty. This meant Ukraine's laws would be followed when they did not agree with those of the Soviet Union.

In 1991, there was a failed attempt to overthrow Soviet leader Mikhail Gorbachev. During the confusion, Ukraine and several other Soviet **republics** declared independence. On December 1, more than 90 percent of Ukrainians voted for independence. They elected Leonid M. Kravchuk president. Then in 1996, the government passed Ukraine's new **constitution**.

The 2004 presidential election resulted in a tie between Viktor Yanukovych and Viktor Yushchenko. A runoff election declared Yanukovych the winner. However, many people claimed the government had interfered with the election. So, a second runoff election was held. Yushchenko won in December and took office in January 2005.

In 2004, Ukrainians led a protest movement called the Orange Revolution to demand a new, fair election.

Varied Landscape

Ukraine is the second-largest country in Europe. Russia is Ukraine's eastern and northern neighbor. Belarus also lies to the north. Poland, Slovakia, and Hungary share Ukraine's western border. Romania and Moldova lie to the southwest. The Black Sea is south, while the Sea of Azov lies to the southeast.

The country's land is mainly flat, even plains. However, the far north is forested. Also in the north, the Pripyat' River flows through lowlands. The Pripet Marshes, Europe's largest **wetlands**, are along the river. The northeast rises to a low **plateau**.

In the west, the land rises to the Carpathian Mountains. Ukraine's highest point is there. Mount Hoverlya stands 6,762 feet (2,061 m) above sea level.

The Dnieper lowland is in central and eastern Ukraine. Here, the Dnieper River flows. This area rolls gently in the east, flattening out toward the west. More lowlands lie south along the seashores.

Belarus

Russia

Poland

UKRAINE

Slovakia

Hungary

Moldova

Romania

Black Sea

Sea of Azov

Russia

North America

Europe

Asia

DETAIL AREA

Africa

South America

Australia

Antarctica

PRIPYAT' RIVER

DNIEPER RIVER

DESNA RIVER

Chernobyl

Kiev

Kharkiv

DONETS RIVER

CARPATHIAN MOUNTAINS

DNIESTER RIVER

DNIEPER RIVER

Mount Hoverlya

Dnipropetrovs'k

Mariupol'

North

West   East

South

Odessa

Kherson

ASKANIYA-NOVA NATURE RESERVE

CRIMEAN PENINSULA

CRIMEAN MOUNTAINS

Kerch

DANUBE RIVER

Sevastopol'

Feodosiya

The lowlands continue on to the Crimean Peninsula. This piece of land sticks out into the Black Sea along the Sea of Azov. A narrow strip of land called the Perekop Isthmus (IHS-muhs) connects it to mainland Ukraine. The Crimean Mountains rise along the southern part of the peninsula. They sharply drop back to the sea on their southern face.

Ukraine's climate is temperate. It is affected by the Atlantic Ocean. During the summer, the east has much warmer temperatures than the west. It is usually hottest in July. Almost three times as much precipitation, such as rain, falls in the summer months as in winter.

January is the coldest month. In winter, the west is warmer than the east. A few inches of snow fall in the **steppes**. But the Carpathian Mountains may receive several feet of snow.

The Crimean Peninsula has a warmer climate than much of Ukraine. Summer there is hot and dry. The average temperature is about 75 degrees Fahrenheit (24°C). During the winter, it is warm and rainy. Usually, it is about 39 degrees Fahrenheit (4°C).

Rainfall

AVERAGE YEARLY RAINFALL

Inches		*Centimeters*
Under 20		*Under 50*
20–40		*50–100*
40–60		*100–150*
Over 60		*Over 150*

Temperature

AVERAGE TEMPERATURE

Fahrenheit		*Celsius*
Over 65°		*Over 18°*
54°–65°		*12°–18°*
43°–54°		*6°–12°*
32°–43°		*0°–6°*
21°–32°		*-6°–0°*
Below 21°		*Below -6°*

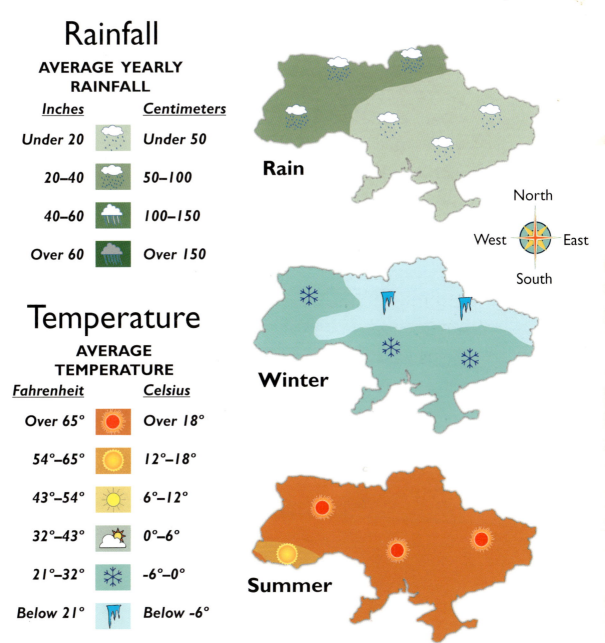

Rain

North
West — East
South

Winter

Summer

Abundant Wildlife

Ukrainian land holds much natural life. The north and northwest contain mixed woodlands. Trees such as oak, ash, maple, pine, linden, willow, and beech grow there. Marshes and peat bogs are also found in this area. However, many of them have been drained and turned into agricultural land.

Much of Ukraine's land has been cleared for farming. Today, the Carpathian Mountains contain the majority of the country's rich forest regions.

Ukraine's central region is a mix of forests and **steppes**. Much of the forested land has become farmland. This is also true in the south. There, many original plants are found in nature reserves, such as Askaniya-Nova.

In the mountains, mixed forests cover the low slopes. Slightly higher up, pine forests grow. Even higher altitudes are covered by alpine meadows.

The Crimean Peninsula's vegetation is distinctive. Both deciduous (dih-SIH-juh-wuhs) and evergreen plants grow in a six-mile- (10-km-) wide coastal area. Nearby, the Nikitsky Botanical Garden grows plants from all over the world.

About 350 bird species live among Ukraine's trees and grasses. People often see owls, partridges, gulls, black grouses, and hazel grouses. Birds such as wild geese, storks, and ducks also **migrate** in Ukraine.

Foxes, wildcats, martens, and wolves hunt the land. Roe deers, elks, wild pigs, and a type of sheep called mouflon also live there. They share the land with rodents such as field mice, gophers, and jerboas. The country's rivers and seas are home to more than 200 fish species. Pike, perch, sterlet, and sturgeon all swim in Ukrainian waters.

Ukrainians

Most people in Ukraine have Ukrainian backgrounds. About one-fifth of the population have Russian roots. A small number of Belarusians, Bulgarians, Moldovans, Poles, and Crimean Tatars also live in Ukraine. In addition, Ukrainians live abroad in countries such as Russia, Moldova, Belarus, Poland, Romania, the United States, and Argentina.

The people mostly speak the country's official language, Ukrainian. In the past, the Soviet Union made Russian an official language. Ukrainian was considered the language of peasants. But today, the people of Ukraine take pride in their language. And, the government respects the languages and **cultures** of the nation's **minorities**.

Life in Ukraine is based on family. Generally, a family is made up of parents and one or two children. Extended family is also important. Frequently, grandparents live with their children and grandchildren. If not, grandchildren usually visit their grandparents for a few weeks during the summer.

Ukrainians who live in cities usually own or rent small apartments. Unfortunately, many of them are in Soviet-era high-rise buildings that were poorly constructed. And, many buildings are overcrowded. City air is often polluted, too.

About one-third of Ukrainians live in rural villages. Small houses are common there. Frequently, these homes don't have modern conveniences such as electricity, running water, or gas for heat. Many village residents are farmers, timber workers, or craftspeople.

Rural homes and villages dot Ukraine's beautiful landscape.

Ukrainian meals include vegetables, dairy products, potatoes, and breads such as sour rye. Pork, beef, chicken, fish, and sausage are popular meats. Tea and coffee are favorite drinks. Fresh fruits such as pears, plums, apples, melons, and berries are also well liked.

A common meal is borscht. This is a soup made of beets, cabbage, potatoes, carrots, and sometimes meat. *Holubtsi* is a main dish made of cabbage leaves stuffed with meat and rice. Crepes, pancakes, and stuffed dumplings called *varenyky* are also favorites. And chicken kiev is known worldwide.

Despite Soviet limitations on religion, many Ukrainians kept their beliefs. About half are **Orthodox** Christians. Others are Ukrainian Greek Catholics or **Protestants**. A small number of Jews live there as well.

Education is important to Ukrainians. Children must attend school from ages 6 to 15. Then, students may study specific careers at specialized schools. Or, they may enter job-training programs. But, many go on to high school for two more years to prepare for university. Kiev, L'viv (luh-VEE-oo), and Kharkiv (KAHR-kuhf) all have major universities.

Plum Dumplings

- 1 cup cold mashed potatoes
- 2 teaspoons melted butter
- 2 eggs, slightly beaten
- 1 teaspoon salt

- 2 cups flour
- water
- pitted plums
- cinnamon and sugar, mixed

Combine potatoes, butter, eggs, and salt. Add flour and enough water to make a soft dough. Lightly knead the dough, cover it, and let it stand. Meanwhile, fill the center of each plum with the cinnamon and sugar mixture. Cut the dough in two parts and shape each part into a 1.5-inch- (3.8-cm-) wide roll. Cut each roll in .5-inch (1.3-cm) sections and flatten each one. Wrap one flat piece around each plum, sealing the edges. Drop dumplings into boiling water and cook until they are puffy and float to the top. Serve with cream or sprinkle with sugar.

AN IMPORTANT NOTE TO THE CHEF: Always have an adult help with the preparation and cooking of food. Never use kitchen utensils or appliances without adult permission and supervision.

LANGUAGE

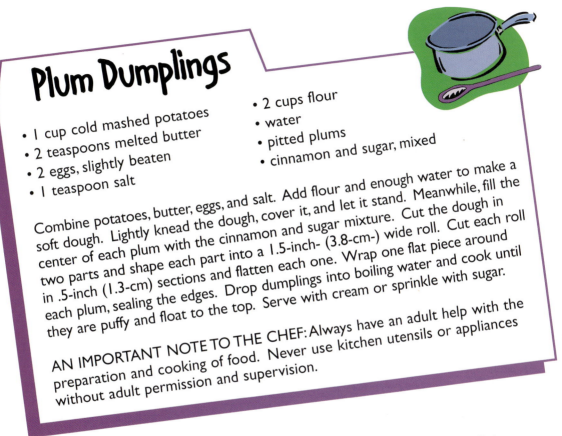

English	Ukrainian
Hello	Привіт (pruh-VIHT)
Good day	Добрий день (DAH-bruh dehn)
Good-bye	До побачення (dah pah-BAH-chehn-nyah)
Please	Будь ласка (bud LAH-skah)
Thank you	Дякую (DYAH-ku-yu)

Growing and Building

After independence, Ukraine suffered from **economic** problems. Since then, the economy has been improving. Still, much of the industrial and agricultural machinery is outdated.

Today, industry is the largest part of the economy. Ukraine produces steel and iron, making metalworking one of its largest industries. Machine-building companies also employ many Ukrainians. Mining equipment and vehicles such as cars, ships, airplanes, and railcars are commonly made goods.

Mining is another important part of Ukraine's economy. Miners remove coal, natural gas, and iron ore from the ground. They also mine manganese, nickel, titanium, and salt.

Ukrainians have produced energy using coal, natural gas, and petroleum for many years. In the 1980s, **nuclear** power became common. Despite the Chernobyl disaster, nuclear plants still produce about one-third of Ukraine's energy.

Throughout history, agriculture has been important to the Ukrainian economy. Farmers commonly grow wheat and sugar beets and raise cattle and hogs. Their farms also

Ukraine is one of the most productive agricultural regions in the world. So, it became known as Europe's "breadbasket."

produce barley, corn, rye, and tobacco. The fishing industry is also **economically** important. Ukrainian ships travel the nation's rivers, the Black Sea, and the world's oceans.

About one-fourth of Ukrainians work in services such as education, health care, engineering, transportation, scientific research, and trade. The country's main trading partners are China, Iran, Turkmenistan, Germany, Poland, Russia, and the United States. Ukraine mainly exports coal, construction equipment, manufactured goods, sugar beets, and wheat.

Cultural Centers

Ukraine's capital, Kiev, lies on the Dnieper River. It is the nation's political, **cultural**, and **economic** center. This north central city is a main hub for roads, railroads, air travel, and shipping. Kiev has several museums and theaters. And, many people study at its universities and research institutes.

In Kiev, old and new exist side by side. The Golden Gate of Yaroslav the Wise and the Cathedral of Saint Sophia have stood for nearly 1,000 years. Underground burial tunnels run beneath the Monastery of the Caves. The Mariinskyy Palace, built in the 1750s, is another well-known sight.

Ukraine's second-largest city, Kharkiv, lies near the Russian border in the northeast. It is a main junction for the country's railroads and highways. Industry is important there, as is education. Kharkiv's university was built in 1805.

Kharkiv is home to the Pokrovski Cathedral from the 1600s. The Uspenski Cathedral has an impressive 294-foot (90-m) bell tower. Freedom Square was built in the 1920s. The city zoo is nearby. Kharkiv also has a planetarium.

Dnipropetrovs'k (duh-nyeh-pruh-pee-TRAWFSK) is Ukraine's third-largest city. Located on the Dnieper River, Dnipropetrovs'k is one of the country's largest industrial centers. The people use the river as a power source. And, the city supports a large iron and steel industry.

The city's schools specialize in mining, agriculture, medicine, metals, and engineering. Dnipropetrovs'k is home to a concert hall and several theaters. People also like to visit Shevchenko Park, named for Ukrainian poet Taras Shevchenko.

The Monastery of the Caves overlooks the Dnieper River. Downstream, the river passes through Dnipropetrovs'k.

Staying Connected

The Ukrainians have built a large transportation system. More than 100,000 miles (160,000 km) of paved roads connect the main cities and towns. About one-third of Ukrainians drive their own cars or motorcycles. In rural areas, bicycles are common.

In the cities, people often use public transportation such as buses, streetcars, and trains. Kharkiv and Kiev are two of the largest railroad centers. These cities have **subway** systems, too. Kiev, Kharkiv, and Odessa have major airports.

The Black Sea and the Sea of Azov have vital shipping ports at Odessa, Kherson, Feodosiya, Kerch, and Mariupol'. For river shipping, the Dnieper, Pripyat', Desna, and Danube rivers are important.

To stay connected without travel, Ukrainians telephone people or mail letters. And, more than 5 million Ukrainians log on to the Internet. To get news, they watch television and read newspapers. News is often influenced or controlled by the government or political groups.

The Ukrainian National Information Agency provides official news about the country's **economy**, **culture**, and sports. Broadcasts are mostly in Ukrainian and Russian. Agencies such as Respublika and the Rukh Press also provide news. The largest daily newspapers are the *Pravda Ukrainy*, *Democratychna Ukraina*, and *Silski visti*.

Ukraine's ports and waterways are important for both shipping and recreational travel.

An Independent Nation

Ukraine is a **republic**. It has a **democratic** system of government. The **constitution** was adopted in 1996 and revised in 2004. It allows citizens 18 and older to vote in elections.

Ukraine's one-house **parliament**, the Supreme Council, makes the country's laws. Ukrainians directly elect representatives to fill half of the council's 450 seats. The other half is appointed based on the number of votes each political party receives in an election. All representatives serve five-year terms.

The prime minister leads the Cabinet of Ministers. Together, they handle daily government operations. They also have the power to introduce legislation to the parliament.

The people elect a president for a five-year term. This is the highest executive office. The president signs laws passed by the parliament and is in charge of the military.

District courts, or people's courts, are the foundation of Ukraine's court system. They decide local matters. Regional

Ukraine's parliament building is located in its capital city, Kiev.

supreme courts deal with broader issues. The **Constitutional** Court decides the constitutionality of laws. The highest court is the Supreme Court. It supervises judicial activities. The Supreme Council elects this court's judges to five-year terms.

For local government, Ukraine is divided into 24 regions called oblasts. Two cities, Kiev and Sevastopol', have special **status**. Like oblasts, they have their own local governments. And, the Crimean Peninsula is considered a self-governing **republic** inside Ukraine.

Celebrating the Seasons

In Ukraine, holidays and festivals honor people and history. The year's celebrations begin with New Year's Eve. People decorate fir trees for the holiday. Parties start in the evening and last until morning.

In spring, Easter is important to many Ukrainians. People observe the holiday by staying up all night either at home or at church. They also ring church bells and light bonfires. An old tradition is to make *pysanky*. These painted eggs feature

bright colors in geometric designs, flowers, or animal figures. Special cakes called *paskha* are another traditional part of the holiday.

On February 23, some Ukrainians still celebrate Soviet Army Day as a kind of men's day. Then on March 8, Ukrainians celebrate International Women's Day. Women receive flowers and gifts and get the day off from work. May 9 is Victory Day, which remembers the end of **World War II**. Independence Day is August 24.

Toward the end of summer, people of the Carpathian Mountains hold the Hutsul Festival. They sing, dance, play music, and light a large bonfire. The Kolomyika and Boikivska Vatra festivals are in August and September. During these celebrations, people sing short, rhythmic folk songs called *kolomyikas*. There are thousands of these little songs!

The Christmas season begins with a special Christmas Eve dinner. It features bread called *kolach*, boiled wheat with poppy seeds and honey called *kutia*, and a fruit drink called *uzvar*. During this season, groups of people go caroling. Others put on a special puppet theater called *vertep*.

Visitors can see numerous **pysanky** *at the egg-shaped Pysanky Museum in Kolomyya, a city in the Carpathians.*

Athletes and Artists

Ukrainians enjoy many pastimes. Chess is a common choice for quiet time. Many people sing in choruses or perform in dance groups. In some cities, Ukrainians spend time in **culture** and recreation parks. These gardens and wooded areas have theaters, lecture halls, and playgrounds.

Folk dancing originated with holidays and festivals. It is still popular at special events today.

Many Ukrainians vacation at the Black Sea. There, they can sit in mineral springs or swim. The Carpathian Mountains are popular for camping. People also visit forest parks near cities to picnic, hike, swim, and even cross-country ski.

Ukrainians still use former-Soviet facilities for practicing soccer, gymnastics, volleyball, hockey, and ice-skating.

Ukrainian athletes have been successful. Figure skaters Viktor Petrenko and Oksana Baiul both won gold medals at the Olympic Games. And, Kiev Dynamo has long been one of Europe's best soccer teams.

Beyond everyday entertainment, folk **culture** is still a part of the people's lives. Weaving is an old art. And, colorful embroidery is often used to decorate national costumes. For this, different regions have their own designs. In the Carpathian Mountains, artists carve detailed designs in wood.

Throughout history, Ukraine has been home to many famous composers. Today, Ukrainians sing folk ballads, as well as historical songs. Sometimes, they are accompanied by instruments such as the *bandura*. This instrument has 50 or more strings. Ukrainians also perform the lively *hopak* folk dance.

For hundreds of years, the bandura has been used to accompany songs praising Ukrainian culture.

Visual art traditions began to grow in about 900. Ukrainian religious icons became well known throughout the region. Some of the beautiful **mosaics** and frescoes from this time are still in Kiev's Cathedral of Saint Sophia. Engraving, sculpture, and portrait painting developed in the 1600s and 1700s.

In the 1800s, Ivan Trush and Mykola Burachek created famous **impressionist** paintings. Oleksander Novakivsky and Alexis Gritchenko are known for **expressionist** pieces.

Ukrainians continued to create art despite limitations during Soviet times. Aleksandr Archipenko sculpted using

Poet Taras Shevchenko is also considered the "Father of Modern Ukrainian Painting."

cubism and other experimental styles. He was important to European art during the 1900s.

Literature is also important in Ukrainian **culture**. Historical works date back to the 1000s. Ukraine's most celebrated poet is Taras Shevchenko. He lived from 1814 to 1861. Collections such as *Kobzar* contain his poems about Ukrainian history.

Other outstanding authors include poet Lesya Ukrainka and journalist, novelist, poet, and play writer Ivan Franko. Nikolay Vasilyevich Gogol is known for his novels and short stories in the Russian language. A more recent favorite is Valerii Shevchuk. He is best known for his novel *Try lystky za viknom*, or *Three Leaves Outside the Window*.

Since Ukraine's independence, other authors have prospered. Oksana Zabuzhko has written popular poetry, fiction, and essays. Salomea Pavlychko is famous for her critical works. And Oleh Lysheha's poetry is enjoyed throughout the world. These and other works give people a glimpse into Ukraine's rich culture.

Glossary

alliance - people, groups, or nations joined for a common cause.

Bolshevik - a member of a political group that came to power during the Russian Revolution. The Bolsheviks became known as communists.

communism - a social and economic system in which everything is owned by the government and given to the people as needed. A person who believes in communism is called a communist.

constitution - the laws that govern a country.

cubism - an art movement developed in the early 1900s. Objects are represented by cubes and other geometric forms.

culture - the customs, arts, and tools of a nation or people at a certain time.

czar - the title given to a Russian ruler who had power before the 1917 revolution.

democracy - a governmental system in which the people vote on how to run their country.

economy - the way a nation uses its money, goods, and natural resources.

expressionist - of or relating to an art movement of the early 1900s. Artists attempted to show how their inner feelings affected what they saw.

famine - a severe scarcity of food.

impressionist - of or relating to an art movement developed by French painters in the late 1800s. They depicted the natural appearances of objects by using strokes or dabs of primary colors.

migrate - to move from one place to another, often to find food.

minority - a racial, religious, or political group that is different from the larger group of which it is a part.

mosaic - a picture or a pattern made by decorating a surface with small pieces of differently colored material, such as glass or stone.

nuclear - of or relating to the energy created when atoms are divided or combined.

Orthodox - a Christian church that developed from the churches of the Byzantine Empire.

parliament - the highest lawmaking body of some governments.

plateau - a raised area of flat land.

Protestant - a Christian who does not belong to the Catholic Church.

radioactive - of, caused by, or showing radioactivity. Radioactivity is the rays of energy or particles given off when certain atoms of certain elements break apart.

rebellion - an armed resistance or defiance of a government.

republic - a form of government in which authority rests with voting citizens and is carried out by elected officials, such as those in a parliament.

Russian Revolution - two uprisings in 1917, during which the czar of Russia was overthrown and a communist government took over.

status - a position or a rank based on comparison with others.

steppe - any large, flat plain without trees.

subway - an electric railroad that runs beneath city streets.

United Nations - a group of nations formed in 1945. Its goals are peace, human rights, security, and social and economic development.

wetlands - low-lying land that collects water and stays damp at least part of the year.

World War II - from 1939 to 1945, fought in Europe, Asia, and Africa. Great Britain, France, the United States, the Soviet Union, and their allies were on one side. Germany, Italy, Japan, and their allies were on the other side.

Web Sites

To learn more about Ukraine, visit ABDO Publishing Company on the World Wide Web at **www.abdopublishing.com**. Web sites about Ukraine are featured on our Book Links page. These links are routinely monitored and updated to provide the most current information available.

Index